Laughter for the young at heart

You're No Spring Chicken

By ED FISCHER

𝓂 Meadowbrook Press

Publication information for *You're No Spring Chicken*

Cartoons, captions, and text by Ed Fischer
Cover and interior design by Koechel Peterson & Associates Inc.,
Minneapolis, Minnesota

Published by: Meadowbrook Press
                 6110 Blue Circle Drive, Suite 237
                 Minnetonka, Minnesota 55343

MBP ISBN 13: 978-0-88166-536-9
S&S ISBN 13: 978-1-4169-5337-1

Printed in the United States of America
15   14   13   12   11   20   19   18   17   16   15   14   13   12   11

YOU'RE NO SPRING CHICKEN PROVES THERE IS A FUNNY SIDE TO BEING OVER 50.

Not just because the cartoons, quotes and anecdotes are genuinely funny, but, as more people are finding out, those over 50 have a keenly developed sense of humor from a lifetime of hard and soft knocks. So, when it comes to achy joints and Social Security and all the other maladies of getting older, it's a little easier to take with the right attitude and a spoonful of laughter.

The fun in this book will make someone's day. Join Ed Fischer and the cream of the world's authors, comedians and statesmen, and next-door neighbors, who have taken a comical and sometimes whimsical look at life's golden years. And as a bonus, share with them a walk down many memory lanes with a collection of elder memorabilia and trivia quizzes.

As someone once said, "It's better to be over the hill than under it." Or as Ed Fischer said, "Just because you're no spring chicken doesn't mean you can't cackle."

To Pearl and Lester —
older, wiser and wittier.

laugh and the world laughs
with you, snore and you
   sleep alone.
          -Anthony Burgess

"When you get older
it takes a lot
longer to do nothing."
             -Catharine Brandt

George Burns attributes his long life to avoiding stress. He says he takes a scissors and cuts all the bad news out of the newspaper before he reads it.

HAPPINESS IS:

Hearing your proctologist say, "You can straighten up now."

– *George Burns*

If I had my life
to live over again
I'd make the same
mistakes, only sooner.

— Tallulah Bankhead

OLD AGE:

– He still chases women...but only
  downhill.

– My wife powers...I puff.

– He says he's 53...and there are very
  few people alive to contradict him.

You're getting old when you feel on Saturday night what you used to feel on Monday morning.

~~

You know you're getting old when...

Your head makes promises your body can't possibly keep.

~~

Over 60 and want to see a puzzled look on someone from the younger generation?

Tell them one of your favorite things to do was to put on your zoot suit to ride in the rumble seat on the way to cut a rug.

~~

A 70-year-old widow went out on a blind date with a 90-year-old man. Returning to her daughter's house around 10:30, she seemed quiet and upset. "What happened?" asked the daughter. "I had to slap his face three times." "You mean...?" began her daughter. "Yes," she answered, "he fell asleep three times!"

Lowell Thomas, introduced to speak at a luncheon, warned the audience that one of the dangers of passing the 80th year of age is that 'everything you say reminds you of something else.'

that reminds me..

But I didn't say anything..

Nostalgia...

The ability to remember yesterday's prices while forgetting yesterday's wages.

–Los Angeles Times Syndicate

Old Timer...

Someone who can remember when bacon, eggs and sunshine were good for us.

– Treasury of Medical Humor, edited by James E. Myers

retirement party
OLD FART
'this is nice - but I was expecting cash'

If you had your life to live over again - you'd need more money.

— Construction Digest

Joe was the type who loved to talk about the good old days. At a movie, he told the girl who handed him his five-dollar ticket, "I can remember when a movie ticket was only fifteen cents." "You're really going to enjoy this movie then, sir," said the ticket girl. "We have sound now."

Health food makes me sick.

— Calvin Trillin

too much garlic?

It takes a long time to become young
—Pablo Picasso

"How can you stand this stuff?" said the grandson to his grandfather, who was listening to 1940s big-band singers. "All they sing about is love and junk," said the grandson. "Well," replied the grandfather, "what's your rock-and-roll music about?" "That's the beauty of it," said the grandson. "Nobody knows!"

Nostalgia is like sex. Every generation thinks it's discovering it for the first time.

- *Michael Barrier*

Money isn't everything, according to those who have it.

– *Malcolm Forbes*

Complete Quiet
as played by nobody

ED FISCH

Youth is a gift
of nature, but age
is a work of art.
– Garson Kanin

First you are young; then you are middle-aged; then you are old; then you are wonderful.

> *– Lady Diana Cooper*
> *(From the book "Gallimaufry to Go,"*
> *by J. Bryan, III)*

THOSE WERE THE DAYS

Girls were babes, dishes, tomatoes, cookies, tootsies; money was scratch; a drunk was a stinko, pie-eyed, fried, tight (as Dick's hatband), plastered.

If you have nothing pleasant to say about anyone, come and sit by me.

> *– Alice Roosevelt Longworth*

A hair in the head
is worth two in
the brush
— Oliver Herford

NEW FRIENDS ON A BENCH
IN A BUSY PARK...

Fred: I can tell you exactly how old you are right down to the month and the year.

Jack: Get outta here.

Fred: I'll bet you five bucks.

Jack: Okay.

Fred: Stand on one leg, raise both arms, open your mouth wide, and cackle like a chicken.

Jack: What?

Fred: Do it. I can tell from that.

Jack: I feel stupid.

Fred: You were 83 last March.

Jack: That's right! That's amazing! How could you tell I was 83 last March?

Fred: You told me yesterday.

One 90-year-old: I got that 60-year-old gal to go out with me.

Another 90-year-old: Wow! How did you do that?

First 90-year-old: I told her I was 80.

Joe claims he's a weightlifter.
Every time he stands up.

One retired grump: Where are my glasses?

The grump's wife: They're on your nose.

Grump: Can you be more specific?

Wrinkles are hereditary.
You get them from your kids.

My personal hobbies are reading, listening to music and silence."
—Edith Sitwell

QUIET
PERSON
ZONE

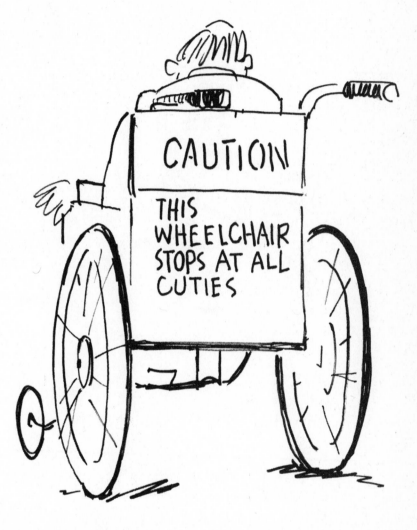

what you can afford on Social Security...

At 71, George was told to make a new friend every six months or so to make up for the friends who may pass away. At 76, he was asked how this plan was working. "Okay," he said, "except now I have too damn many friends!"

～

Old age is not for sissies.

— Joseph H. McGinty

～

One must wait until the evening to see how splendid the day has been.

— Sophocles
(On Old Age)

～

'All of us learn to write in the second grade ...most of us go on to greater things.'

- Bobby Knight

LIFE 101

26

Billie says when she was young it was "Look, but don't touch." Now she says it's "Touch, but don't look."

～

Happiness is good health and a bad memory.

— Ingrid Bergman

～

'It helps to have a rather odd face like mine. people always recognize you.'
-Elsa Lanchester

` George-you forgot the car..!´

The greatest Christmas occurs when a family mixes up the lists of those who sent cards and those that didn't, and send to both to be sure.

THOSE WERE THE DAYS WHEN:

– People sat down to dinner and counted their blessings instead of calories.

– People who wore jeans worked.

– Dirty words in books were dots and dashes.

– Baths were taken once a week and religion every day.

– The hero only kissed the heroine.

– A job was the first thing you went steady with.

– People dressed up for church.

– A baseball game was called on account of darkness.

– Breakfast cereals were silent.

One of the things
nobody ever tells you
about middle age is
that it's such a nice
change from being
young
— Dorothy Canfield fisher

You know you have a problem grandchild when you remove him from church and the congregation applauds.

How to show off a grandchild's photos...

Before you push your cart within arm's reach of the checker at the supermarket, say, "Would you like to see pictures of the grandchildren who will be eating these groceries?"

– Mary McBride

Of course Americans trust in God. You can tell the way they drive.

EARLY CAR NICKNAMES...

Pierce-Arrow - "Fierce Sparrow"
Studebaker - "Steady Breaker"
Duesenberg - "Doozie"

Thanksgiving comes after Christmas for those grandparents who entertain the whole family on Christmas Day.

OLD, OLD, OLD JOKES...

Why does a fireman wear suspenders?

What did the little chicken say when it found an orange in the nest?

When is a door not a door?

When it is ajar (a jar).

Oh, I see the orange mama laid.

To keep his pants up.

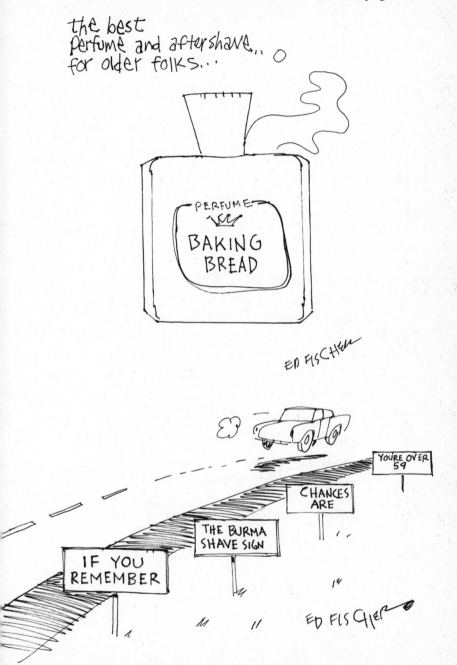

You know someone's had too much coffee when they answer a question before you've asked it.

Kenny, in his late fifties, noticed that senior citizens get free coffee at a local cafe. He asked, "How old do you have to be to be a senior citizen?" The waiter looked at him for a few seconds and without saying a word, poured him a cup of coffee.

Alice was asked by a friend if she ever thinks about the hereafter. She said, "I do all the time. No matter where I am in the house, kitchen, den, upstairs, downstairs, I ask myself, 'Now, what am I here after?'"

I like TV better than the movies - it's not so far to the bathroom.
— Cecil B. DeMille

What a difference a few decades makes. When TV first came on the scene, it was only on the air for a few hours…and half that time was taken up with cowboy chases.

~~

You know you're getting old when you have to sit down to brush your teeth.

~~

If God had to give women wrinkles, why couldn't he put them on the bottom of her feet?

~~

Pundit's advice on getting older…
If you can't recall it, forget it.

~~

From anonymous:
I'm never lonely because I have four men in my life…
I get up in the morning with Charlie Horse.
I spend the day with Arthur Itis.
I dine with Will Power.
I go to bed every night with Ben Gay.

I like long walks, especially when they are taken by people who annoy me.

— Fred Allen

A 70-year-old marries a 20-year-old woman…

The minister: "Do you take this man for richer or poorer…?"

Bride: "For richer."

~~

Life in the modern, fast track:

There was a day when the smell of home-baked bread wasn't just there because you wanted to make the house smell better for a potential home buyer.

~~

Let's hear it for the things that have made our life better…

…like company-recorded phone messages.

…like cheap appliances that last one day longer than the warranty.

…Like 100 TV channels and nothing worth watching!

'I'm a self-made man, but if I had it to do over again, I'd call in someone else.'
— Roland Young

Never go to a doctor whose office plants have died.

— Erma Bombeck

70-year-old Martha's fashion style consists of buying anything that doesn't itch.

Elder Nathan B. claims he eats lutefisk so his wife can find him in the dark.

After age 70, it's just patch, patch, patch.

—Jimmy Stewart

While governor of New York, Teddy Roosevelt held press conferences after running up the seventy-seven steps of the state capitol in Albany. Any reporter who still had the breath to ask a question was given an answer.

Press

puff puff?

~~

Jack points out to his wife's friends, "The jaw muscle is the most powerful and most used in the body."

~~

What do you suppose God had in mind when He created hiccoughs?

~~

The meek shall inherit the grandchildren.

– *Gilbert C. Greenway*

THOSE WERE THE DAYS...

When people weren't mashing, spoon-
ing, necking or pitching woo, they were
saying things like...hold yer hosses!...
Isch Ka bibble...you tell 'em, corset,
you've been around women...my fad-
der's moustache...so's yer old man...
jeez Louise!...that's all she wrote...
get a horse...don't spit, remember the
flood...long time, no see...love me, love
my dog...you tell 'em brassiere, you've
been over the bumps...horse feath-
ers!...pardon my wet glove...Pardon
my wet glove??? You said a mouthful!

'The more the
pleasures of the
body fade away,
the greater to me
is the pleasure
of conversation'
                    - plato

46

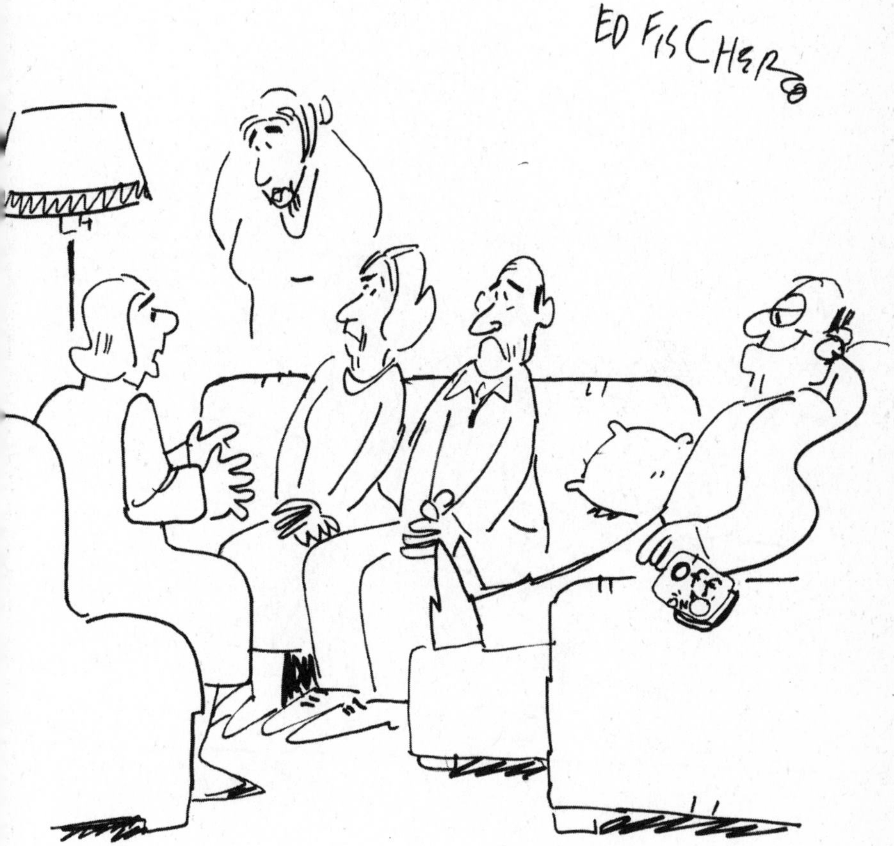
ED FISCHER
OFF
ON

Don't complain that you're not as young as you used to be. You never were.

WHATEVER HAPPENED TO...

Bloomers...bowlers...homburgs...pana-
mas...ascots...cravats...scarfpins...
galoshes...chemises...watch chains...
watch charms...detachable cuffs...
sleeve garters...and a feather in the
hatband? Whatever happened to hats?

When you think that the medical world
knows everything, remember, ketchup
was once sold as medicine.

– Nantucket Inquirer and Mirror

The person most often late for a doctor's
appointment is the doctor.

Various points in time...

Big Bang

Baby Boomer

ED FISCHER

How's that again, doctor...?

Richard Lederer has compiled the following medical observations made by doctors from around the world...

- She has had no rigors or shaking chills, but her husband states she was very hot in bed last night.

- She was divorced last April. No other serious illness.

- I have suggested that he loosen his pants before standing, and then, when he stands with the help of his wife, they should fall to the floor.

- The patient is tearful and crying constantly. She also appears to be depressed.

- Rectal exam is deferred because patient is sitting upright.

- The patient was found to have 12 children by Dr. Blank.

- Many years ago the patient had frostbite of the right shoe.

- The patient is a 74-year-old white female who was brought to the ER (emergency room) by paramedics acutely short of breath.

- The patient refused an autopsy.

- The patient has no past history of suicides.

- Patient left his white blood cells at another hospital.

- Apparently the mother resented the fact that she was born in her forties.

- Physician has been following the patient's breast for six years.

- The patient is a 79-year-old widow who no longer lives with her husband.

- The patient's past medical history has been remarkably insignificant with only a 40-pound weight gain in the past three days.

- The patient is a 71-year-old female who fractured her little finger while beating up a cake.

- She slipped on the ice in early December and apparently her legs went in separate directions.

- The patient left the hospital feeling much better except for her original complaints.

– From Lederer on Language
by Richard Lederer

His birthday has become an annual event at our house – every year or so.

~~~

It's amazing…according to the obituary column in the newspaper, people die in alphabetical order.

~~~

My doctor put his hand on my wallet and asked me to cough.

~~~

I've written 6 books. Not bad for a 96-year-old guy who has read only 2 books.

– George Burns

~~~

He was so old, the candles cost more than the cake.

~~~

The thing about getting old is everything is further away than it used to be.

 at 80, his plan for getting ahead was to stay even.

ED FISCHER

Joe wanted to suggest, tactfully, that his 90-year-old Mom get some help with her chores. "You know, Mom," he said, "there are volunteers that help older people who are in need. What do you think?" "Okay," she snapped back. "If they can't get anyone else, I'll help them out for awhile."

Then there's Mary of St. Paul, Minnesota, who sometimes would take her false teeth out when they felt uncomfortable and wrap them in a napkin. The problem was, they were often thrown out with the garbage, where Mary would search and retrieve them. One day when she was getting ready to go to church, she couldn't find them again and with the help of her daughter, the search was on. They looked and looked until the daughter suddenly found them...in Mary's mouth.

'With me, a change
of trouble is as good
as a vacation.'
    —David Lloyd George

Grandchildren today are handled differently than they were in years past...

It used to be children were spanked. Nowadays they're taken to a pediatrician who refers them to a counselor.

Kids used to get watches for their high school graduation. Now children wear them to kindergarten.

Kids used to turn off the TV so they could do their homework. Now they just tape the programs on a VCR.

~

...And grandmothers do things that set them apart from other people...

A grandmother...

Feels her grandchild's opinion should be respected, even before he can talk.

Lets a grandchild take a nap on a $500 bedspread.

Laughs heartily at a grandchild's remarks about Grandma being so old.

– Mary McBride

YOU KNOW YOU'RE GETTING OLDER WHEN...

...The gleam in your eye is from the sun hitting your bifocals.

...You feel like the morning after the night before, except you haven't been anywhere.

...You decide to procrastinate, but then never get around to it.

...You look forward to a dull evening.

...You sit in a rocking chair but can't get it going.

...Dialing long distance wears you out.

...A fortune teller offers to read your face.

The future just isn't what it used to be.

One thing about being bald – it's neat.

~~

By the time we realize our parents were right, we have children who think we're wrong.

– Guillermo Hernandez

~~

Ever notice that you have to get old before people start saying how young you look?

– Joey Adams

~~

The secret of happiness is to count your blessings and not your birthdays.

– Shannon Rose

You're old enough to be a grandma if...

Someone calls you spry.

You decide to get a job and discover all of your references on your resume are deceased.

The things you talk about to your doctor take more than one sheet of paper.

After becoming a grandparent, you need reality therapy for grandmas who think their grandchild is perfect.

Faith is something entirely possessed by children and they don't know they have it.
-Ed Howe

REMEMBER WHEN...

– There was no place to go where you shouldn't?

– "Come again" was painted on the back of the "welcome to" sign of a town?

– If you didn't know what was going on...probably nothing was?

– The only place open all night was the mailbox?

– The only place air-conditioned was the movies?

Getting old is merely a matter of feeling your corns more than you do your oats.

– Henny Youngman

I am not afraid of tomorrow, for I have seen yesterday and I love today.

– William Allen White

*Elaine from Ely, Minnesota,
tells this story:*

There was an explosion at a local senior citizen's center and 50 of the group died and went to Heaven. St. Peter apologized that Heaven was full and they would have to go to Hell temporarily until space opened up. After a month, an angel came to St. Peter and said: "We'd better do something about getting those seniors back up to Heaven." "Why?" asked St. Peter. "Because," the angel said, "they've held several bake sales and have raised the money to buy a large number of air conditioners."

～

One thing about getting old is that you know all the answers, but nobody asks the questions.

～

there are times when forgetting can be as important as remembering — and even more difficult

—Harry and Joan Mier, `Happiness begins before breakfast`

Name the singers from years past.

1. _____ Starr
2. Rosemary _____
3. Ink _____
4. Julius _____
5. Les Paul and Mary _____
6. _____ Holliday
7. _____ Ekstein

Answers:
1. Kay
2. Clooney
3. Spots
4. LaRosa
5. Ford
6. Billie
7. Billy

TODAY:

5 people watch a 27" TV screen

1950:

27 people from the neighborhood watched a 5" TV screen.

~~

YOU'RE OLD WHEN...

...you begin to think, gee, 65 isn't so old.

...your idea of unwinding is going to bed.

...you, ah...ah...you forget what you were going to say next.

~~

Visiting the Social Security office for the first time is like the first day of school when you were a child. You feel like you don't belong there, but there isn't much you can do about it.

– Pearl Swiggum

~~

Old is when you look the food over instead of the waitress.

If I had my life to live over again,
I would start going barefooted earlier
in the spring and stay that way later
in the fall. I would play hookey more.
I would not work much to get good
grades except by accident. I would ride
on more merry-go-rounds. I would eat
more ice cream and less beans.

– Nadine Stair, age 85

'It's not the days
of your life that
count, but the life
in your days'
-Adlai Stevenson

In the hospital, Joe told his long-time wife he was feeling much better since the operation except for this bump on the back of his head. "Oh, that," said his wife. "They ran out of anesthetic."

~

Just because your doctor has a name for your condition doesn't mean he knows what it is.

— Arthur Block

~

A Norwegian grandma's favorite dinner-time saying: "*Eat, drink and be quiet!*"

~

The early bird never gets to see the 10 o'clock news.

~

How is it...some 70-year-olds can polka for hours but can't bend over to pick up a gum wrapper?

~

We're living in an age of specialists and statistics. 4 out of 5 doctors recommend another doctor

In Bosque mysticism they greet people by embracing them and giving them five metaphors…

∿

What to say to an older person who is very special to you…

You are the look and smell of lilacs in the spring.

You are the aroma of freshly baked bread.

You are the taste of hot, homemade chicken soup on a fall day.

You are the warmth of an Amish quilt on a Minnesota winter night.

You are the sound of silence, a fresh breeze and the feel and smell of clothes just off the clothesline.

∿

`Only through love can we attain communion with God.´
    —Dr. Albert Schweitzer

Days we'll never see again...

...When a Christmas present for under $5 was enough to keep a kid busy for weeks.

...Free glasses with a fill-up of gas.

...A 3-cent stamp.

...Double feature movies with selected short subjects.

If only I still had...

...My 1939 Plymouth.

...My decoder ring.

...My daughter's first Barbie doll (worth a fortune).

...The chance to buy that lakeshore lot for $2,000 that now sells for $30,000.

~~

BASEBALL NOSTALGIA...

...The bottle/bat...Joltin' Joe...the rabbit ball...Shoeless Joe...Mudville... Casey...(at bat and Stengel)... the balloon ball.

Name the TV shows of the past...

1. Howdy _____...with

2. ... _____The Clown

3. This Is Your _____

4. Queen For A _____

5. My Little _____

6. Our Miss _____

7. Kukla, Fran and _____

Answers:
1. Doody
2. Clarabell
3. Life
4. Day
5. Margie
6. Brooks
7. Ollie

A man is usually bald four or five years before he knows it

-Ed Howe

A particularly deaf elder was bragging about his new hearing aid. "It's great," he said to a friend. "I now can hear the birds singing and the crickets chirping. I can hear a conversation a full block away." "You don't say," said his friend. "What kind is it?" The proud owner consulted his wristwatch and said, "Twenty minutes after two."

– Bennett Cerf

One old curmudgeon loved to tell the story of his 68-year-old brother who, as his final circus act, shot himself out of a cannon 4 times larger than any cannon ever used before. "Jeez Louise!" exclaimed his friend. "How did he withstand the shock of that?" "I don't know," said the old-timer. "They haven't found him yet."

What did Jimmy Durante say at the end of his shows?

Remember these commercials…?
1. I'd walk a mile for a _____
2. Ask the man who owns one.
3. Only her hairdresser knows for sure.
4. I can't believe I ate the whole thing.
5. Call for _____

5. Phillip Morris
4. Alka-Seltzer
3. Clairol
2. Oldsmobile
1. Camel

Answers: "And good night, Mrs. Calabash,
wherever you are."

Why is it that the person who snores is always the first one to fall asleep?

A woman asked George Burns, "Is it true you still go out with young women?" George said, "Yes, it's true." She said, "Is it true you still smoke 15 to 20 cigars a day?" George said, "Yes, it' s true." She said, "Is it true you still take a few drinks every day?" "Yes," George repeated, "it's true." "Well," she said, "What does your doctor say about all this?" "I don't know," Burns said. "He's dead."

It is now proved
beyond doubt that
Smoking is one of the
leading causes of
statistics

—Fletcher Knebel

Old, Old Observation...

It blewed so hard, they was whitecaps
on granmaw's pisspot.

> *Spring Hope, N.C.*

∿

WWI and WWII Stuff:

Zeppelins...Tommies...Big Bertha...
Spitfires...The Hun...Fokkers and
Sopwith...Tokyo Rose...White Cliffs
of Dover...Loose Lips Sink Ships...
Ration Cards...Sergeant York...

∿

And the Songs...

How You Gonna Keep 'Em Down on
the Farm? • Pack Up Your Troubles in
Your Old Kit Bag • Roses of Picardy •
When Johnny Comes Marching Home •
My Buddy • Bugle Boy of Company B •
Oh, How I Hate to Get Up in the
Morning • Over There • Tipperary •
We'll Hang Out Our Washing on the
Siegried Line

Whatever happened to fifty-cent pieces?

A Friend of Mildred's Observes:

Mildred laughs at everything since she got her new teeth.

∿

How old would you be if you didn't know how old you was?

– Satchel Page

∿

Football Nostalgia

...drop kick...the flying wedge...nose-guards...the Bumerooski...the Statue of Liberty play...Johnny Unitis...the Galloping Ghost...the Four Horsemen

∿

Where but radio would you find people like Rochester, Titus Moody, Mrs. Noosebaum, Charlie McCarthy, and lines like..."It's a joke, son!" "Howdy Bub" and all that stuff falling out of McGee's closet?

∿

George's friend, Mike, says George has a photographic memory. It's just, Mike says, that sometimes he forgets to take the cap off.

He was bald and a shining example.

~~

There was the bronze age, the iron age, and, for the over fifty, the metal age: gold in the teeth, silver in the hair and lead in the pants.

~~

Alf's wife was so neat, every time he got up to go to the bathroom, she made the bed.

~~

Lois chooses younger men. At her age, there are no older men.

~~

Mary suffers from CRC:
Can't Remember Crap

~~

What's wrong with being absent-minded? Think of all the new people you meet over and over and over...

~~

`A good laugh is sunshine in a house.`

—William Makepeace Thackeray

'Nothing so needs reforming as other people's habits.'
—Mark Twain

Remember these quiz shows?

Fill in the blanks...

1. What's My _____

2. I've Got A _____

3. You Bet Your _____

4. The _____ Question

96

Two can live as cheaply as one, but for only half as long.

~

Mee of Little Canada, Minnesota, noticed on a coupon for quilted toilet tissue that it was "100% recycled bathroom tissue." "Some things just shouldn't be recycled," says Mee.

~

One 68-year-old:
   "Have I shown you pictures of my grandchildren?"

His 70-year-old friend:
   "You haven't, and I've been meaning to thank you."

~

Flight...

Remember the Spirit of St. Louis, Enola Gay, the Flyer, the Spruce Goose and the Voyager? But what about the Tingmissartog?

Tingmissartog was the plane Charles and Anne Lindberg flew to the Arctic and the Orient.

`Let there be spaces
between your
togetherness/And
let the winds of
the heavens dance
between you`
—Kahil Gibran

*Remember these great comic
strips?*

Fill in the blanks...

1. The Yellow _____

2. Maggie and _____

3. Mutt and _____

4. _____ Abner

5. _____ Nemo

6. Bringing Up _____

7. Katzenjammer _____

Answers:
1. Kid
2. Jiggs
3. Jeff
4. Li'l
5. Little
6. Father
7. Kids

'If a dog jumps in your lap, it is because he is fond of you; but if a cat does the same thing, it is because your lap is warmer'

—Alfred Noth Whitehead

~~

Grandmother Mary McBride says, tongue-in-cheek:

To get your grandchildren to go to bed when you're babysitting, tell them the jails are full of kids who don't go to bed on time.

~~

The comfort of being 59 is that you now know that you're too old to die young.

You know you're getting old when your wife asks you to pull in your stomach, and you already have.

Grandma: Let's have some yogurt.
   Can you spell yogurt?

Kid: N-O W-A-Y

∿

BOOK TITLE BY LOIS WYSE:

Grandchildren are so much fun, I
should have had them first.

∿

Make up what you don't remember.

– *Georgia B. Watson*

∿

George remembers his humble begin-
nings, of course; that's all he can
remember.

∿

65-YEAR-OLD YUPPIES I KNOW:

He was healthy, wealthy and wise-
cracking. She wasn't as wise as an owl,
but she was always a hoot.

Over 50 quiz... What's a...

1. Middy?
2. Whippet?
3. Snoose?
4. Moniker?
5. Long Johns?

We don't know one millionth of one percent of anything
—Thomas Edison

Answers:
1. Blouse with sailor look
2. Car
3. Chewing tobacco
4. Nickname
5. Long underwear

ED FISCHER

LOOK ON THE BRIGHT SIDE:

No matter how old you are, you're younger than you'll ever be again.

You're old when you consider the ten o'clock news the late, late show.

The early bird gets the worm,
The snowbird gets the heck out of town.

Nowadays the only way to get a doctor to make a house call is to marry one.

Growing old has one advantage. You'll never have to do it again.

She's so old, her Social Security number is 7.

At Steve's age, when a woman flirts with him at the movies, she's after his popcorn.

Death bothers Woody Allen, because, he muses, if the soul is immortal and lives on after the body, he's afraid his clothes will be too loose fitting.

He: I slept like a log.
She: More like a sawmill.

If Patrick Henry thought that taxation
without representation was bad, he
should see how bad it is with representation.

> *– The Old Farmer's Almanac*

I'm proud to be paying taxes in the
United States. The only thing is –
I could be just as proud for half the
money.

> *– Arthur Godfrey, 1951*

Up to forty, it's all luck.
From forty to sixty, it's a little luck.
After sixty, it's all maintenance.

the only way to
solve the traffic problems
of this country is to
allow only paid for
cars on the streets
and highways
-will Rogers

Anybody who has ever used the expression, "It was no Sunday School picnic" has obviously never been to a Sunday School picnic.

—The Parish Chute

How do you disperse a threatening crowd?
Take up a collection.

— The Joyful Noiseletter

There are two ways a sermon can help: Some rise from a sermon greatly strengthened, others wake up greatly refreshed.

— The Joyful Noiseletter

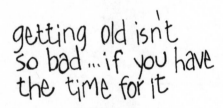

85-YEAR-OLD SVEN:

There is scientific proof that birthdays are good for you. The more you have, the longer you live.

~~

An elder's view...
I miss those "wing" windows next to the windshield on car doors.

~~

Sick Jokes...

Patient: Doctor, doctor, I swallowed a bone.

Doctor: Are you choking?

Patient: No, I'm serious.

~~

Al's wife: It's strange. Joe fell off a 20 ft. ladder and was in bed for a week.

A friend: Why is that strange?

Al's wife: He fell off the bottom rung.

An archaeologist is the best husband a woman can have. The older she gets, the more he is interested in her.

> – *Agatha Christie*
> *(Who married an archaeologist)*

∿

As infectuous as a yawn.

> – *Baltimore*

∿

Someone asked the 80-year-old countess of Essex, "When is a woman done with sex?" She answered, "Ask someone older than me."

∿

Maturity is realizing that being a bird-brain is okay especially when it means flying south for the winter.

> –*L. Lovstad*

∿

Kid: Who's that lady on the treadmill?
That's no lady, that's my grandma.

> – *Lois Wyse*

NOWADAYS...

Over the hills and through the woods to Grandmother's condo we go...

∿

In the dreams of children are the hopes of grandparents.

— Lois Wyse

∿

Retire? What could I retire to?
What else am I going to play with?

— Duke Ellington

∿

You're officially old when you finally get to the stage where people no longer say, "Gee, you don't look old enough to be a grandparent!"

∿

Fun is like life insurance. The older you get, the more it costs.

— Kin Hubbard

historians are still trying to convince us that the united states was founded to avoid taxation

She was approaching forty, and I couldn't help wondering from what direction.

—*Bob Hope*

Charlie has gone from R&R to N&N: Nipping and Napping.

RADIO:

Television with the picture tube blown.

You know you're old when someone asks you what a "running board" is.

George Burns says he can't die.
He's booked.

From an old Farmer's Almanac: Old age was creaking up on her.

Way back, knowing who had money was simple. All you had to do was count the holes in a person's Buick.

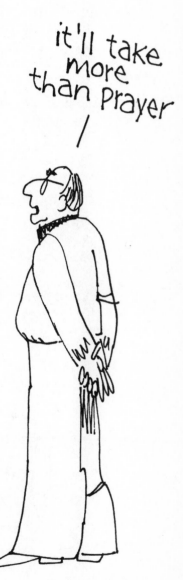

We do not remember days; we remember moments.

—*Cesare Pavese,*
"The Burning Brand" (Walker)

An expert is someone called in at the last minute to share the blame.

—*Sam Ewing in "Mature Living"*

Motel mattresses are better on the side away from the phone.

—*age 50*

Expensive silk ties are the only ones that attract spaghetti sauce.

—*age 54*

ED FISCHER

If today was a fish, I'd throw it back

Those Were the Days. Remember...

"The crank-out or fold-down front windshield...chains and studded tires...
a knob attached to the steering wheel
(usually with a picture of a rose or a
pretty girl in it)...glass packs?

Things of the Past:

78's
WPA
8 Tracks

*What did Dave Garroway say at the
end of his TV program?*

Answer: "Peace."

When I am an old woman, I shall wear
purple with a red hat which doesn't go
and don't suit me. And I shall spend my
pension on brandy and summer gloves
and satin sandals and say we have no
money for butter…I shall go out in my
slippers in the rain and pick the flowers in
other people's gardens and learn to spit.

– "Warning" by
Jenny Joseph